NATIONAL GEOGRAPHIC

Nature's SOLUTIONS

PATHFINDER EDITION

By Leslie Hall and Phyllis Edwards

CONTENTS

Nature's SOLUTIONS

By Leslie Hall

People like to make things work better, faster, and cleaner. Luckily, they can turn to nature for some great ideas.

WE CAN LEARN A LOT FROM THE NATURAL WORLD. Just think about it—nature always seems to work smoothly and **efficiently**. Plants and animals don't waste energy, and they are specially designed to live in balance with their environment. That's why engineers and business people are turning to nature for solutions to people's everyday problems.

PROBLEM: How can we help athletes swim even faster?
SOLUTION: Look closely at a shark's skin.

Even the sports world has solved problems by imitating nature. To help athletes swim faster, swimsuit developers used **biomimicry**. They analyzed the motions of some of nature's very best swimmers—sharks.

It turns out that a shark's skin is covered with scales shaped like teeth. These "teeth" have tiny grooves between them. When water passes over a shark's body, it is channeled through these tiny grooves. Because the water flows through the grooves instead of passing over or around them, there is less friction, or resistance. The water moves freely over the shark's skin like a wide, fast-moving river.

With this in mind, engineers created a swimsuit with grooves that mimicked those on a shark's skin. Swimmers who wore the suits swam faster than they had ever swum before, and even broke records.

Bird Beaks and Bullet Trains

PROBLEM: How can we build quieter and more efficient trains?
SOLUTION: Copy the shape of a bird's beak.

Kingfisher birds are perfectly designed to catch fish. To capture their prey, they plunge headfirst into lakes and rivers, diving so neatly that when they enter the water, there's almost no splash. Their quiet, stealthy dives help them catch fish by surprise.

This gave a Japanese engineer named Eiji Nakatsu an idea. He helped design the Shinkansen bullet train, one of the fastest trains in the world. When the train was first launched, it zoomed along at speeds up to 300 kilometers (186 miles) per hour. The speed was great—it was everything people had hoped for. What wasn't so great was the noise the train made when it came roaring out of a tunnel.

Nakatsu used what he knew about the kingfisher bird to solve the problem. He knew how smoothly a kingfisher is able to enter the water, with its long, sharp beak. So Nakatsu redesigned the front of the train using the kingfisher's beak as a model. This new **approach** paid off: with its new shape, the train moves more quietly and uses less electricity!

Gecko Grip

PROBLEM: How can we build machines that climb walls or move across ceilings?
SOLUTION: Study a lizard's tiny toes.

Geckos are pretty amazing lizards. They can run up and down walls, and even hang upside down from ceilings. It doesn't matter if the surface is rough or smooth, wet or dry. Nothing keeps geckos from sticking around.

Their sticky secret isn't super strength. It isn't even super glue. The secret is the tiny hairs that cover their feet and toes. Each hair splits between 100 to 1,000 times. This means that geckos can hold on to a surface at a billion different points! Geckos have another secret tool. The ends of the hairs are shaped like spoons, giving the lizards an iron grip.

Engineers studied these terrific toes to make a robot called Stickybot. Stickybot uses a material like the hairs on the gecko's toes. It can climb up smooth walls and defy gravity, but it is not nearly as fast or agile as a gecko. Still, engineers are constantly working to improve Stickybot, and people hope that one day it will help with search-and-rescue missions.

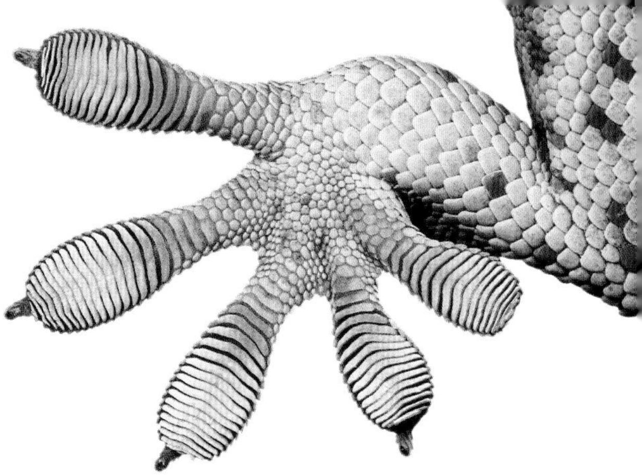

Fancy Feet. *Scientists studied geckos' toes to make a robot that can climb up walls.*

Sleek Shape. *The shape of a kingfisher's beak inspired the front end of this bullet train.*

Lessons From Leaves

PROBLEM: How can we keep the outside of buildings clean?

SOLUTION: Study how rainwater rolls off a leaf.

The leaves of a lotus plant look waxy and smooth, but they aren't. When you look at the leaves under a microscope, you see tiny bumps all over them. These bumps are the plant's secret tool for staying clean and dry.

How do the bumps work? When a raindrop falls on the leaf, the bumps keep most of the water from ever touching the surface of the leaf.

More importantly, the bumps make the water bead up into ball shapes, instead of spreading out. The drops can't stick to the leaf, so they roll right off, carrying dust, dirt, and bacteria with them. This is how lotus leaves keep themselves clean. Engineers **researched** this process, and then created a type of paint that can clean itself. Dirt rolls right off the paint just like it rolls off a lotus leaf.

Engineers are also trying to copy the way the leaf stays waterproof, and they are hoping to find **applications** for this ability in business. Someday, for example, we may be able to thank the lotus leaf for helping us keep ice off airplane wings and car antennas. Lotus lessons are even being used to keep clothes dry.

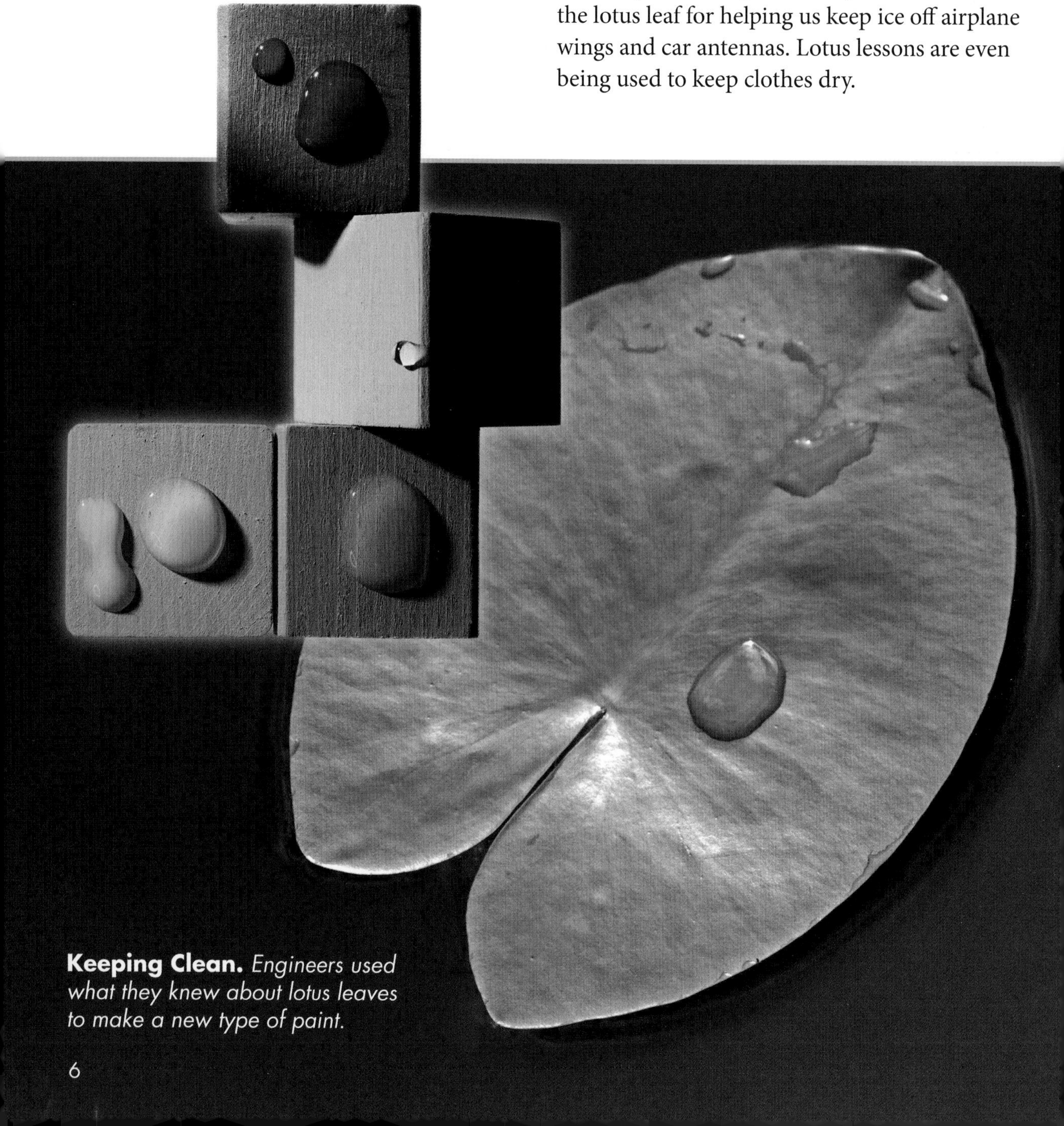

Keeping Clean. *Engineers used what they knew about lotus leaves to make a new type of paint.*

Ideas Taking Flight. *Engineers study bombardier beetles to build better jets.*

Beetle Juice

PROBLEM: How can we re-start a jet engine while the plane is flying?
SOLUTION: Do what some beetles do.

It may seem odd, but a tiny beetle has helped jet engineers. That's because clever engineers figured out how to make a better jet engine by studying what bombardier beetles do.

The beetles shoot hot liquid at predators such as ants. It all starts with the gases in the beetle's abdomen. When a beetle feels threatened, the gases move into a small chamber in its abdomen.

In the chamber, the gases create large amounts of heat and pressure. When the pressure is great enough, boiling-hot liquid and steam shoot out of the beetle's body.

So what does this bug have to do with jet engines? At cold, high altitudes, jet engines sometimes shut down, and pilots need to turn them on again quickly. Engineers want to build jet engines that pilots can reignite easily in mid-air. That's where the beetle comes in.

Engineers are studying the beetle to see how it makes and shoots out the hot spray so quickly. If they can copy the beetle's process, they can send fuel into the plane's combustion chamber more effectively. The tiny beetle is also inspiring new types of car engines and even better fire extinguishers.

Fuel-Saving Fish

PROBLEM: How can we build cars that use less gasoline?
SOLUTION: Look closely at the shape of a fish.

When engineers want to figure out how to make cars that use less gasoline, they usually turn to math formulas and calculators. The engineers at one car company, however, decided to try something different. They studied the boxfish, a fish with a square shape that lets it move through the water smoothly. The engineers then mimicked the fish's keel-like fins and overall shape in a sleek new car design. The result was an aerodynamic car that uses less fuel.

Would you like to build a better car, or a faster swimsuit, or a quieter train? Do what the animals do. These examples of biomimicry are just the beginning. Get out in the natural world, look around, and ask questions. Then start searching for solutions. Which creatures will inspire you?

WORDWISE

application: a way to put something to use

approach: a way to get close to something

biomimicry: imitating nature to solve problems

efficient: does not waste energy

research: to get information about something

Flying Snakes Help Build Better Aircraft

BY
PHYLLIS EDWARDS

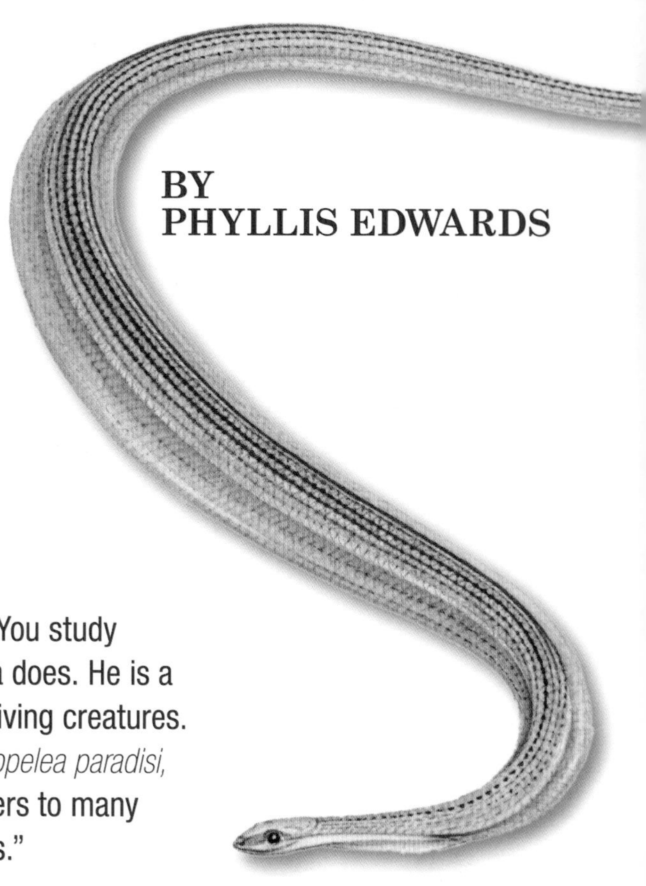

How do you design a better gliding aircraft? You study flying snakes, of course! That's what Jake Socha does. He is a professor of biomechanics, or the movement of living creatures. He has studied the paradise tree snake, or *chrysopelea paradisi,* for many years. His research has revealed answers to many questions about the unique way this animal "flies."

Meet the Paradise Tree Snake

While there are quite a few species of flying animals, *chrysopelea paradisi*, the paradise tree snake, is the champion. It is able to leap from one tree branch to sail overhead to another tree several yards away! It is more efficient at navigating through the air than flying squirrels, flying lizards, or flying fish. Only birds are better at flight than the paradise tree snake.

The term "flying snake" is not quite accurate, though. This reptile does not flap wings to push itself through the air. And although it is able to manipulate its body to achieve longer air time and greater distance, it cannot gain altitude. Therefore, it is more accurate to say that the paradise tree snake glides.

But that doesn't seem possible! If you drop a rope from a tree branch, you know that the rope will fall directly to the ground. So you would expect a rope-shaped animal to do the same. How can this animal not only stay airborne and travel some distance from its starting-place, but also control its flight to a certain extent? These are some of the questions that Jake Socha set out to answer.

All the Right Moves

Jake Socha has spent many hours watching *chrysopelea paradisi* fly and recording their flights on film. Many of Socha's photographs and videos at National Geographic websites answer key questions about the mystery of this species' ability to fly.

Socha found that the paradise tree snake performs several surprising movements during its flights. First, the snake does not fall downward from a branch and then start to fly. It actually leaps from the branch horizontally so it can begin its flight from the highest possible point. It dives toward the ground for a few seconds to gain speed and then levels out to glide to a landing.

Perhaps the most amazing feat Socha observed, however, is that the snake seems to control the direction of its flight. It undulates its body, moving it from side to side as if slithering across the air. This undulation helps the snake stay aloft for a longer flight. Socha also noted that the snake seems to select a specific place to land and steer its flight toward that spot.

A Snake in Flight

Leaping from branch → *Diving to gain speed* → *Undulating to stay aloft and control direction*

Flying Facts

Species: *Chrysopelea paradisi*
Class: reptile
Size: Up to 4 feet long

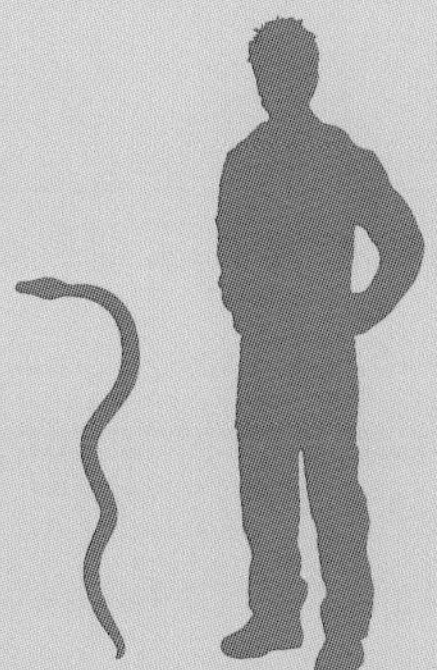

Range: Southeast Asia
Habitat: treetops in Southeast Asia
Diet: carnivorous: rodents, small lizards

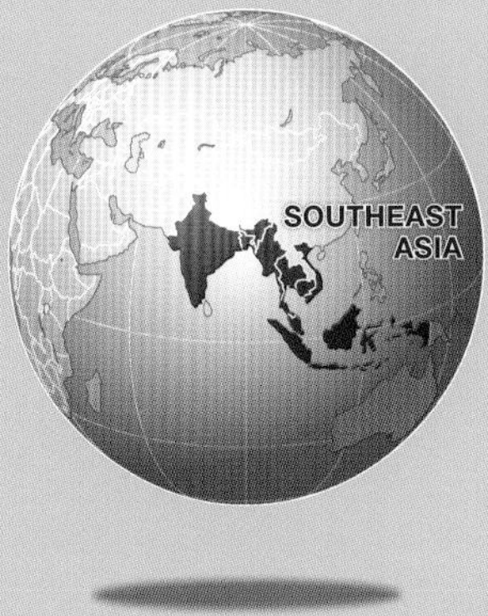

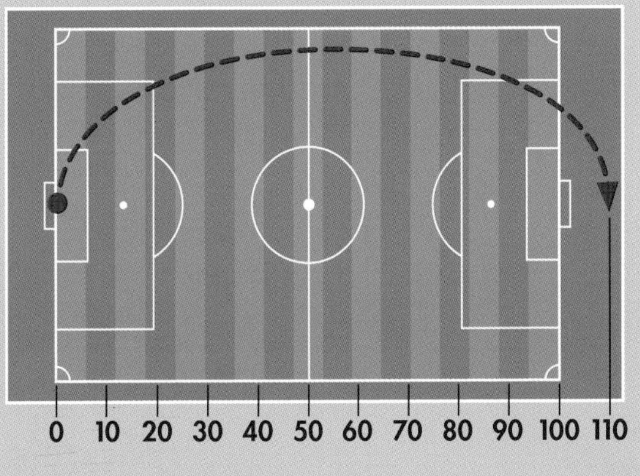

Gliding Distances: up to 330 feet, or 110 yards
Flying Snake's Path: 110 yards
Soccer Field: 100 yards

Challenges and Responses

Why do paradise tree snakes glide? All wild animals share a big problem: predators! If a large bird hovers too close by, the flying snake can confuse the predator by relocating several yards away. If a giant, snake-hunting lizard climbs up the snake's tree, gliding away to a far-off tree is an excellent solution for the snake.

Most importantly, all animals also face the challenge of finding enough food every day. What if you were ready for a meal and were stuck high up in a tall tree? If you were an ordinary snake, you would have to climb down the tree, slither across the ground, and climb up another tree to find dinner. That would take a lot of time and energy! When a paradise tree snake is hungry, if it doesn't find a tasty morsel in one tree, it can glide off to another tree to grab a bite to eat.

The Future of Flight

Will people use what we have learned about flying snakes to change the way we build gliding aircraft? Think about the cross-section diagram of a snake's body in flight and then visualize an image that resembles a space ship.

What if we hooked dozens of these shapes together into a snake-shaped string? It would look like a flying train! Will people travel on such a train in space someday? Only time or maybe more studies of *Chrysopelea paradisi* will tell.

Flying squirrel

Key Questions

Jake Socha has found answers to these key questions.

1 ***Exactly how does a rope-shaped animal "fly"?***

You can imagine how other gliding animals manipulate their body parts to achieve flight. The flying squirrel, for example, uses its legs and extra skin to create "wings."

But a snake doesn't have legs or any other limbs. The solution is amazingly simple—the snake uses its skeleton to change the shape of its whole body from the inside out!

2 ***How does this shape help the snake stay aloft?***

To find out, researchers combined photographs of a snake in flight with images that shows how air flows around the snake's body. They found that the combined image looked a lot like a diagram of an airplane wing.

Both the wing of an airplane and the gliding snake's body have a shape called an airfoil; the shape that keeps an object airborne. The snake's entire body is like a long, narrow wing!

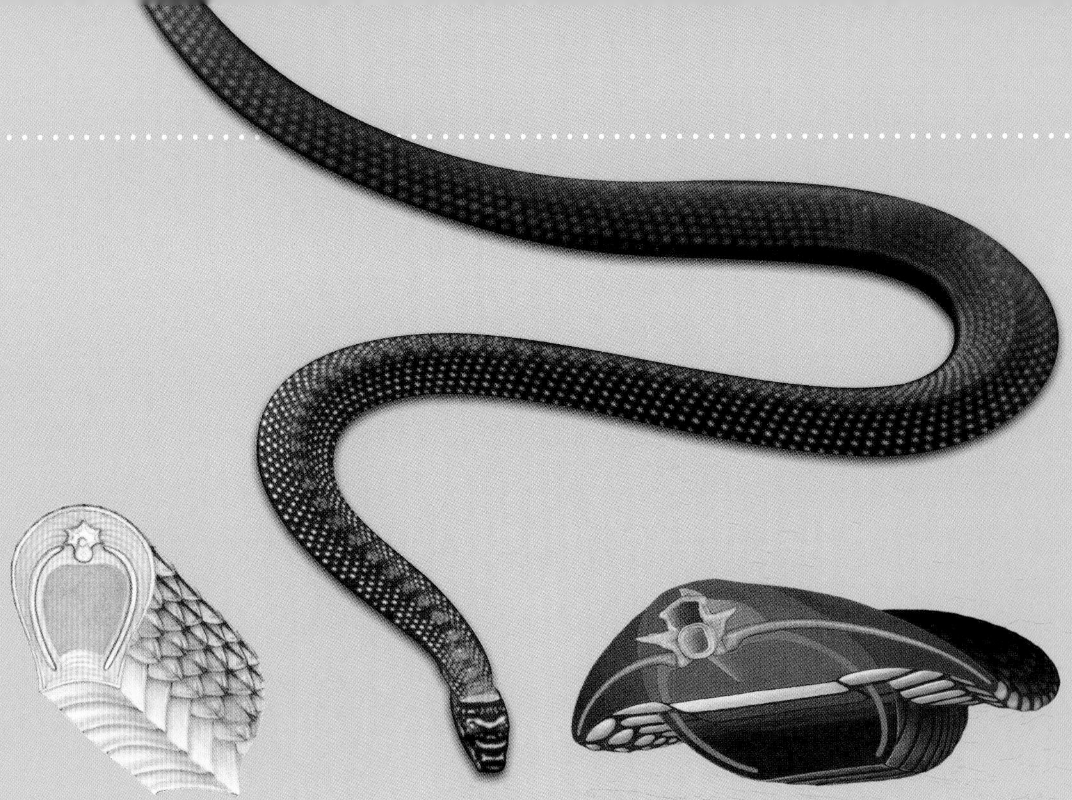

Not Flying. *When it is not gliding, the snake's body is shaped like a long, round tube, a bit like a garden hose.*

Flying. *To "fly," the snake extends its ribs outward from the center of its body to form a concave shape. It looks like the snake has sucked in its stomach!*

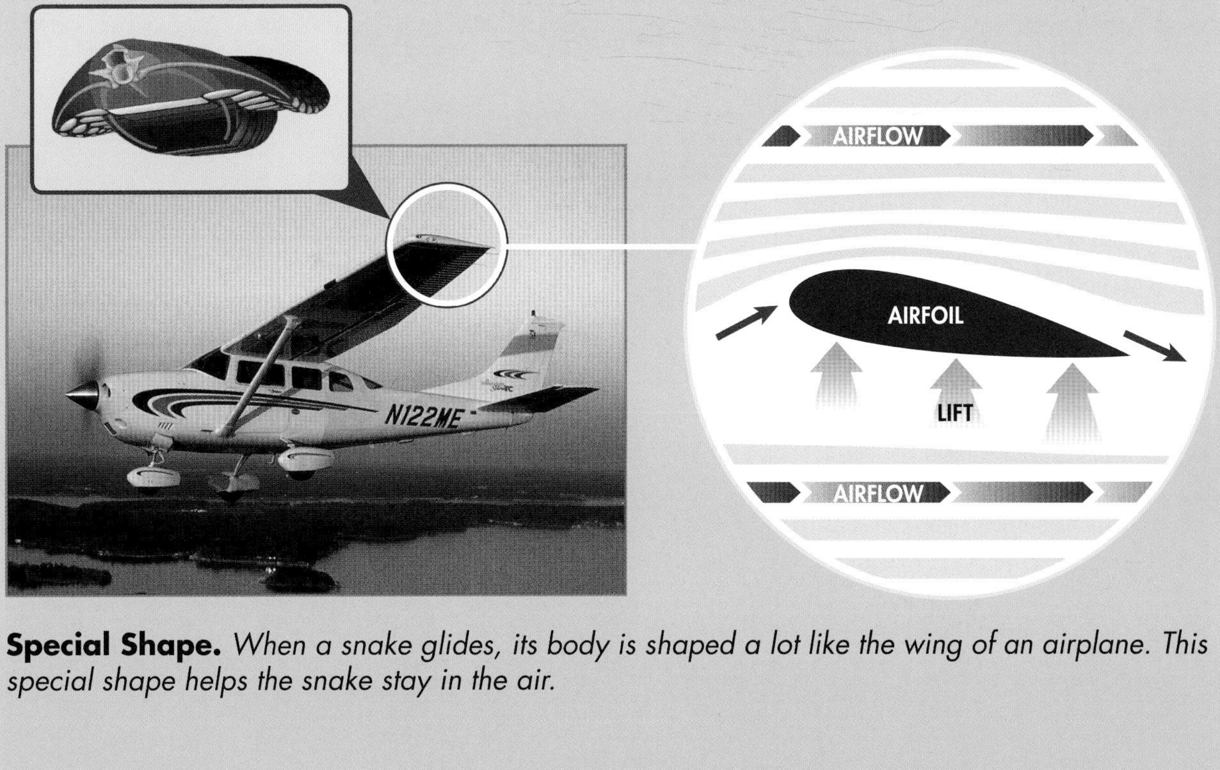

Special Shape. *When a snake glides, its body is shaped a lot like the wing of an airplane. This special shape helps the snake stay in the air.*

Wild Ideas

Time to let your ideas about biomimicry run wild. Then answer these questions.

1. What makes plants and animals efficient?
2. How does biomimicry help engineers and business people?
3. Name three ways people apply what they have learned from biomimicry.
4. How does the paradise tree snake fly?
5. How does Jake Socha learn about paradise tree snakes?

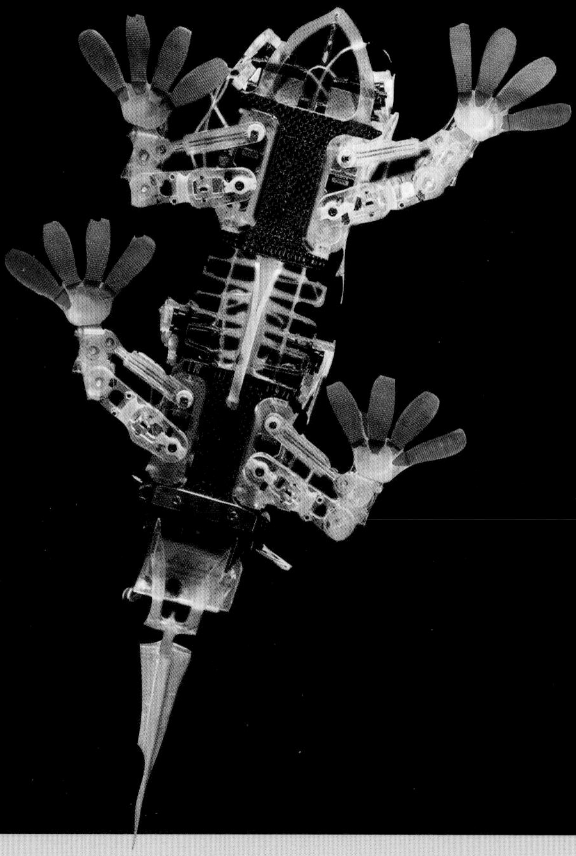